Cherie

Let Christ
carry your
imagination
away.

The *Heart* of a Man
A Collection of Poetry

Love
David

12/5/97

The *Heart* of a Man
A Collection of Poetry

ISBN: 1-57502-663-5
Library of Congress Catalog Number: 97-91704

Manufactured in the United States
10 9 8 7 6 5 4 3 2 1

To order additional copies of this book, send $7.00
+ $3.00 for shipping and handling (for each book) to:

PENGUINS UNLIMITED
P. O. Box 2072
Yelm, WA 98597
(360) 458-0935

Printed in the USA by

MORRIS PUBLISHING
3212 East Highway 30 • Kearney, NE 68847 • 1-800-650-7888

Table of Contents

Every Heartbeat

Remembering Mother

Father's Eyes

Satan's Chamber

Friendships Forever

Mystical Creations

His Gifts

Knots in this Family

Miscelaneous

Foreword

It has been our distinct honor to know David Rossman for some years now and he has been blessed by God with an unusual talent--that of communicating truth through words in a most powerful way.

David has experienced in his life, more than most, much pain and rejection, yet this has refined him into a true man of God, a man who can indeed write first-hand about, "The Heart of A Man."

This is a book that we can heartily recommend and know it will have deep impact on all lives of the readers that have the privilege of reading and partaking David's anointed writing.

----Dan and Norma Wooding, Founders
ASSIST Ministries
P. O. Box 2126
Garden Grove, CA 92842-2126, USA

Dedication

Jesus Christ
For the gift of writing
I give Him all the praise

My sons, Joshua and William
For the two tries at fatherhood
This doesn't make up for the lost time, I know.
No matter how many miles or time are between us,
I will forever love and miss you.
May the Lord bring us together again.

My family and friends
Who helped me through it all

My late mother
Beverly J. Rossman
For teaching me enough to know that
a handicap doesn't always show, even if it is physical.
I love you!

Acknowledgments

Gina Ronhaar, my eighth grade English teacher at
Marble Falls Junior High, Marble Falls, Texas
it was in your class that it all began.

A special thanks to Dan, Norma and Les at the
ASSIST
(Aid to Special Saints in Strategic Times), for
their constant support, encouragement and prayer
that I would one day see my words in print.

My wife, Donna, for the countless
proof-reading and editing.
How or why she puts up with me, I'll never know.
God knows, and for that I am truly thankful.

Janine, thanks for the push to go forward
with my ideas.

God Bless to all.

Every Heartbeat
(Romance the mind)

"A Chase For Love At Night"

In the dead of night the shadows fall. The time is right. Your body's hot, but your heart is cold, as we run into the night. You tear my heart, turn away, then watch it break. I gather the pieces in my hand. The time is now, to take a stand. I've heard enough. I've lost control. I love you with my heart and soul.

You took what you could, but you didn't take it all. With the thought of a chance and the will to fight. I'll chase you through the night. You cut like a knife with the sharpness of your eyes. You took my body by surprise. Now that have you, I'll never let you go. If there's something to hide, you must let me know. Together we can let the power of love shine in the night.

You're a friend of a friend. I had to know you. We fell in love and moaned with passion. Our grips tightened as the fire flared. Our bodies blend, trembling and excited. Under the cover of darkness our hearts soared. Daylight was coming and that we feared.

To the savage streets we took. With every step came an over the shoulder look. Forget what they've said, we'll show them all. 'The bigger they are, the harder they fall'. When the night turns to day, you may turn me away, but our hearts will fight. You know, we'll never outrun the night. Hold me forever. We will stand and fight. We were strangers. Fools of the light as we try to outrun the night.

"A Rose Shaped Friendship Made of Crystal"

A rose
In the midst
Of all daisies
Your friendship
As the beauty
Of the rose
Overcomes all else
For you could bring me smiles of sunshine
Over all the tears that
Fall from my heart
As the pedals of the rose
Bloom outward
Our friendship shall blow ever stronger in God's
wind
I may not know you as well as some think they do
But what I see and what I know
Is all that I need to know
As the lightning flashed
Some friendships are trashed
But our friendship
I pray
Is one that will last
As long as life itself
I shall value our friendship as though it were crystal
Set on a shelf up high
Waiting to be broken
With this in mind
I'll treat our friendship with every bit of tenderness
I can find

"As Time Goes By"

I need you,
You need me.
Together we'll be free.
We'll fly away,
On a wing,
And a prayer.
Babe, I'll always be here.
As long as you are,
I'll show no fear.
And with this love,
That knows no barriers,
We'll go far.
I hope you'll,
Help me through.
All the good times,
And the bad.
The happy ones, And the sad.
Filled with love,
We'll be the carriers.
I love you so much.
That's not a little,
But a bunch.
We'll live forever,
In harmony,
And in love together.

છ3જ

"Captured"

The home in which,
My heart does live.
Has the love,
I wish to give.
I also wish,
For you to take,
The love my heart,
Does make.
I live on a cloud,
In the sky.
I look into your eyes,
To find,
Them full of,
Wonder and amazement.
One touch from you,
Numbs my body.
My heart was caught,
In your hand.
Now, by your side,
I'll forever stand.

"Don't Walk Away"

Do you remember when,
Life was simple,
And plain to see?
It's easier to pretend.
Close the door,
And then turn the key.
We're living and hoping,
Laughing and trying.
Life without you,
Would be,
A life of crying.
So don't leave me alone,
With this feeling inside.
For it's only in you,
I can confide.
Don't walk away!
Don't leave me as you found me,
In a world wrapped around me.
Only dreaming and sighing.
Life without your love,
Is only worth dying.
When you're in my arms,
My heart's really flying.
Come to me,
Don't walk away!
Give me the choices,
Of living and hoping,
Laughing and crying,
Touching and feeling,
Dreaming and dying.
Life without you,
Is a life without love.

"Fire Eyes"

Your eyes,
Are a blazing blue flame.
And I am to blame.
For all that has been done.
'Cause you are the one.
My heart slows down,
When you walk into sight.
My heart beats,
In the heat of the night.
You make me notice,
The thing called love,
That is symbolized,
By a dove.
Your eyes burn in the dark,
To light our way,
As we walk through the park.
Down deep inside,
Of my eternally burning fire,
My heart burns with desire.
You told me of,
The love that dies,
But whatever happens,
You'll always be my,
FIRE EYES!

"Holding You"

Holding you...

I can tell this feeling is true.
If I may hold you,
For one more day,
I'll be forever thankful.
For this I pray.
Hold me now and forever;
And I promise your heart,
I'll never sever.
My love for you,
Shall be forever true.

"In Spite..."

IN SPITE...
Of the way we were;
When we were together,
I'll always care for you.

IN SPITE...
Of the way;
You treated me,
I'll always love thee.

IN SPITE...
Of the fact;
That you were so young,
You'll always be the one.

IN SPITE...
Of the way;
You feel today.
I'll always feel,
The way I did,
When I moved away.

"Left Alone"

I don't know what to do,
When I'm not with you.
Things just aren't the same,
As they were,
When our love,
First became.
When I think of you,
All I see,
Is a blur.
No longer what,
Was to be.
I wonder why,
You said good-bye.
When you turned,
And walked away,
My heart died.
All that echoed in my head,
Were the last words you said:
"You'll forget me,
· Just give it time."

"Live - N - Love"

I live in sadness,
I live in vain.
I live in happiness,
I live in pain.
I'll love my family,
I'll love my friends.
I'll love my life
Until it ends.
I'll live my life,
In the Lone Star state.
I'll live right here,
Until I seek the Heavenly Gate.

"Love and It's Life"

Love won't start,
Until you light the spark.
Once the fire starts,
It will turn the hearts,
Into burning flames of passion.
Some love,
Can bring you,
Heartaches and tears.
Remember...
Love is like a rainbow,
It won't end,
Unless you end it.

"Love Is Blind"

Love is blind...
When you're
In Love,
Faults are what
You won't find.
Love is like
A shield.
When you're
In Love,
It blocks out
The truth,
And lets in
The lie.
If you don't
Believe me,
Look into my eyes.
There you will see,
The tears,
I cry.

"Love At First Sight"

I met you at a most unlikely place
We were strangers for that moment
I didn't realize at the time
But it was love at first sight

Your hair, golden blonde
Glistened in the sunlight
Your voice
As soft as the pedals
Of a rose
Your eyes, dark
They hold a passion-a-fire

What I didn't see then
I see now
The time we spend apart
Only makes me love you more

We were strangers then
But this is now
Now is today
I'll always love you from afar
Tomorrow is another day
And if ever 'now' becomes 'then'
I'll love you in a whole new way
Thanks to love at first sight.

"My Love"

Though my love,
Is far away.
Though my love,
Is but a myth.
I'll dream of her,
Both night,
And day.
Though she is,
Much younger than me,
With her memory,
My heart,
Shall be set free.
Her life will go on,
As mine surely dies.
Until the day,
When we are as one.
The pain prolongs,
As long as,
I hear her cries.
It makes my heart,
Lay in vein.
It hurts worse,
With the mention,
Of her name.
She may forget,
The memory of me,
But I will forever cherish,
And love,
The memory of she.

"One Night Only"

Show me the love,
You hold inside.
When you're with me,
There's nothing to hide.
Together our love,
Will grow over all.
Without you,
My love will fall.
As night comes on,
The passion grows strong.
As day breaks,
That golden dawn.
That special love,
Is gone.
Though for that time,
Your heart was mine.
It is now,
I draw the line.

"Shadow"

You're the fading shadow...
In the memory,
Of my past.

You're the fading shadow...
That will never last.

You're the fading shadow...
I tried to hold,
But never could.
When I got near,
I looked into your eyes,
And saw a tear.

You're the fading shadow...
That turned and walked away.
I heard the words,
Which weren't "hello" or "hi".
Instead they were the words,
"Good-bye."

"Someone"

Someone to care,
And always be there.
Someone to hold me near,
And wipe away the tears.
Someone who will make me laugh,
When I cry.
Someone to help me strive for life,
When I want to die.
Someone who will love me,
For who I am.
Not for whom I'm made out to be.

"Strength of A Wife"

Roses are for you,
He is, too.
Take care of him,
He needs your love and tenderness.
Your lives will spring high.
Up there it will shine.
You vowed your lives forever and always.
Your mind fills with happiness,
Your heart with love.
From time to time,
A tear may flow,
That shows how far your love will go.
Everyone has a weakness,
Strengths as well.
When his ego is hurt,
You become his power.
Stick by him,
He needs you.
You're his life.
Give him your heart.
You are his wife,
For life.

"Strength of a Husband"

Building with bricks of love,
Communication and trust.
Marriage can be a dream,
But reality is a must.
You're the candle,
That burns of reassurance, security,
Warmth and love.
She's the dove,
Willing to settle beneath a stronger wing.
May the future,
Shine with beauty and grace.
May the past,
Be not a fading glimmer of light,
But of memories and joy,
Built to last.
Remember...
Love is fragile,
Not a toy.

Two Become One
July 25, 1994

The Spirit of God and His giving of love to unite the two as one hovered within the church as family members gathered, waiting for the wedding to take place.

At Five, the wedding began.

The best man looked proud to be a part of this joyous occasion, waiting to hand the ring to the groom.

The groom stood tall, dressed in a charcoal gray sport coat and tie. A smile beneath his neatly trimmed mustache, shown the joy and love he felt. Calmly he waited beside his wife-to-be. She, in her white lace dress and joyful smile, looked so beautiful standing by him, as she would through life, in the presence of God and all who shared in this day. Her blonde hair glistened as it cascaded down over her shoulders. She was nervous as all could see, by the way her bouquet of pink carnations and daisies shook as she held it. The maid-of-honor stood by in black and white, smiling.

The viewers watched, just moments before the music filled the church. A vast silence danced above the gatherers. Everyone eyed the bride as she came to be one with the groom.

There They stood, the groom and his bride, holding hands as they exchanged the looks that say, "I love you." The pastor began to read the Scripture that would lead to the words of holy matrimony.

From the videotape that was later watched, it was made known that the groom as well as the bride, had a very hard time holding back the tears of joy that were brought on by the wonderful music that was played. It was also seen that the bride, with her voice as soft as that of a baby's coo, said the words that everyone could barely hear, "I will."

When the words, "You may now kiss the bride" came out of the Pastor's mouth, everyone clapped as the groom took advantage of his instruction.

That was the day, two separate doves, Brenda M. Peck and James A. Gibson, hovered as one under the Holy Spirit and in front of family and friends. They all knew that their love, along with that of God, would see to it that they live a long and happy life together.

Two Become One
June 11, 1994

The day was hot with nerves and sun. Many eager people waiting for the wedding to take place. The church was dancing with the Spirit of God and His giving of love to unite the two as one.

At Two, the wedding began.

The charcoal gray and teal suit the best man wore made his brown hair stand out. He looked proud to be a part of this joyous occasion.

The ring bearer handed the ring to the groom.

The groom stood tall, dressed in charcoal gray and teal to match. Calmly he waited for his wife-to-be to come down the aisle to stand by him, as she would through life, in the presence of God and all who shared in this day. The viewers sat in the pews, just moments before the music filled the church. A vast silence danced above the gatherers. Everyone turned, seeing the bride led by her two fathers, come to be one with the groom. She in her white sequenced dress and vail of white too, looked so beautiful. Her shoulder-length brown hair glistened. She was nervous as all could see, by the way her white bouquet shook as she held it.

There they stood, the groom and his bride, holding hands as they exchanged the look that says, "I love you." The pastor began to read the Scripture that would lead to the words of holy matrimony.

From the videotape that was later watched, it was made known that the groom as well as the bride, had a very hard time holding back the tears of joy that were brought on by the wonderful music that was sung. It was also seen that the bride, with her voice as soft as that of a baby's coo, said the words that everyone could barely hear, "I will."

When the words, "You may now kiss the bride" came out of the pastor's mouth, everyone clapped as the groom took advantage of his instruction.

That was the day, two separate doves, Tonie Southworth and James Smith, hovered as one under the Holy Spirit and in front of family. They all know that their love, along with that of God, would see to it that they live a long and happy life together.

"Tell Me"

Tell me...
You care,
I'll be there.
Stay by me,
The best,
Is yet to be.

Tell me...
You love me not,
Then I'll leave
Of a lost love,
I'll grieve.

Tell me...
You'll love me.
And those words,
I will believe

"*Thanks...*"

for the love
you were willing to share

for saying
"*I'll always care*"

for the times
we've shared together

for telling me
"*This bond will be forever*"

But mostly thanks...
for being you

"Turn Around, Walk On Forward, Walk Through Time"

Turn around,
And see,
What you left behind.

Turn around,
And see,
What you tried to hold on to.

Turn around,
And see,
What you once knew.

Turn Around,
And see,
That there's someone,
Who once loved you.

Turn around,
And see,
Someone special there.

Walk on forward,
For now there's someone,
Who cares for you.

Walk on forward,
For life will go on.
You are his only one.

Walk through time,
And take It slow.
For inside you,
A child is growing.

Walk through time,
It is the love you share,
That will bring,
Your child here.

Turn around,
   Walk on forward,
Walk through time.
      In love together.

"The Everlasting Rose"

I awoke last night,
To see you in the moon light.
In your hand,
You held a pink rose.

I shook my head,
To clear my thoughts.
What I seen,
Tied them in knots.

You laid the rose,
On my bed.
I sat up,
As it began to glow.

You walked my way,
These words I heard you say:
"This rose I once held,
Is now in your care.
When something goes wrong,
It will be there."

After these words,
You turned away.
Before the sun rose,
To start the new day.

These words you continued to say:
"This rose I give.
Will forever live.
When you look at this rose,
You'll think of me.
It is then
We'll together,
Be set free."

"Who Will Love the Children?"

Who will speak for the children...
The ones left alone?
Who will be the friend to those
Who have no place to call home?

Who will dream for the children...
The ones whose dreams have died?
Who will create a world of hope
From pain and hurt and lies?

Who will cry for the children...
The ones who have no tears?
Who will hold the hands of those
Who hold the hand of fear?

Who will care for the children...
Who have no cares at all?
Who will catch the tiny souls
Who don't care if they fall?

Who will laugh for the children...
The ones taught not to smile?
Who will help to bring them joy
For a few and shortest while?

Who will play with the children...
The ones who work for love?
Who will be the first to say
"I'm sorry" is not enough?

Who will love the children...
The ones who learn to hate?
Who will take the time to care
Before it is too late?

"You're the One"

You're the one,
Whom I do love.
You're beautiful,
And Bright.
You're the one,
I dream of at night.
Though you are there,
And I am here,
We have no need.
To fear.
If it's meant,
For us to be,
As we shall soon see,
when we're together,
We're set free.

Remembering Mother
(Can you see her?)

"Christmas Without You"

Christmas without you
Will be hard this year
For you're not close
But you are near
Tears will fall
This Christmas Day
'Cause four months ago
You went away
I'll remember
Your happiness and
Your joyous ways
From this day on
I'll count the days
Our last Christmas together
Was in '85
When you were here
Awake and alive
I'll hold that time close
Close to my heart
And sadly remember
The day we did part
Now you're in Heaven
God's golden land
He'll take care of you
He'll hold your hand

"Future"

Live in the present
Not in the past
Although they may make you cry
Some memories
Must die
Let loose of your hold
And let that life go
I wish you would live
Where we are
Instead of in your memories
Afar
Live for today
And not for what's gone
You are the only one
Who can set your soul free
Be now in the world
You should be
Come stay with me
And although what lay ahead
May not be pleasant
Look at the future
Positively
And let the past be

"Her Pain Is Mine"

The pain shoots through her
As she lies there in bed;
The pain of worried thoughts
Runs through my head.

I pray, I cry;
In hopes that she won't
Have to die.

Instead of her
I wish it were me;
But the LORD has chosen
Her time is to be.

I walk through school
Like a bumbling fool;

I try my best
But, the thought of her
Won't let me rest.

As she goes through spells
Of fever and chills;
I get the feeling that this isn't fake
But it is for real.

I have pains
Down deep in my heart;
And there are times
I wish they would part.

The LORD taking her
Will make me weak;
Then make me strong.

And although she will be gone
And the tears will flow
Onward my life
Will have to go.

"Memories Never Die"

I now remember, with tears in my eyes
The memory of my mother's words:
     "I am going to die, with only three months to live."
I stood in disbelief, for it was hard to imagine why God would
want to take my mother away from me. But, no matter how
much I wished He wouldn't, He was going to and there was
nothing I could do--but pray.

The sun shone warmly outside, but the silence and the air in
the room grew rapidly thin, black and chilling.

As time went on, her illness became worse. She grew weaker
and thinner and I began to see not the strong loving woman
who took care of me, but a lady who seemed to have aged
many years beyond her youth. She wanted so much to die, for
it would take her pain away.

Her shorted life was lengthened by unwanted hopes for life.
The need to have some care beyond our family's caring was
strong. She was checked into the nursing home near by.

The days were long and warm for those outside our family unit,
but the days for us, were short and cold. The nights were long
and heated with worries.

The hours became days.
The days became weeks.
The weeks became months, as we wished for God to take her
to her life beyond the lives of earthly beings.

I saw her lie quietly in her bed. Her strong arm, now grown
weak, reached out to touch me.

The feeling of her touch was very distant and cold, with a
sense of warm love from the heart. She fell silently into deep
sleep as I left the room.

Each time I saw her, in the weeks that passed, I could smell
the aroma of death coming to take her away from my life. It
was then that I realized that I, at the age of seventeen, would
now be truly alone.

The time came on the first day of August of '86, one year after
her words were first brought to my ears, that the last loving
breath of my closest friend was taken away and along with my
friend went my mother.

"Mom"

You're the best
Better than the rest
You're next to none
For all you've done
Although you're a year older
You've grown a little bolder
You've helped me
When I needed it
And even when I didn't
You caught me
When I stumbled and fell
You were always there
At the sound of a bell
Although things weren't always fair
I knew that you cared

"My Last Letter"

Dear mom,

I've missed you since you passed away. So I thought I'd write and tell you what I had to say.

In December, Mike's getting married.

Eight months and four days after you died, dad was buried.

Jacque has a boy and Tama has a girl. Johnny, Alli and their boys are doing fine. Julie and her kids are too. I wish you could see them. I know you'd love them as much as they'd love you.

I graduated high school and started college in the fall.

Well, I'd better go, but first I want you to know...

Remember when you gave me your ring? You told me to hold it close to my heart until I found that special someone. Well, I did as you said--TWICE.

The first girl took care of it as though it was hers, for she knew it was really yours. We broke up. She gave it back.

Two months later I met someone new. Someone I thought was just like you. I was wrong--all along.

I thought it was going to be all right for the two of us. I gave her your ring. A promise ring as well. We started opening up and started sharing.

Then one night I called her, she said, "Stop caring!" In March we broke up. I don't know why. She wasn't careful with your ring as she was with every other thing.

I'm sorry Mom, for the loss of your ring. It meant more to me then anything. I'll never forgive myself for falling in love. Yet, I still love her. I don't know why. When I think of your ring, I always cry.

Well, I have to go.

I LOVE YOU, Mom.

"Pain and Hurt"

As the shadows of darkness
Cover your life
As the clouds
Cover your skies
Tears fall
From my eyes

As the sea gulls fly high
The sun shines for me
When you're around
Through my eyes
I see the changes in your life

I see the light
Can you see
Or are you held
By the cold arms of night

Please stop and see
What this does to your family
Ask God to set you free

"Shadows of Silence"

As the night's
Shadows of silence
Fall closely
Upon her
While she lay quietly
In her bed
Scrambled thoughts
Trample through my head
I am the last
The last of eight
While the others run
I sit and wait
As for her pain
She takes a pill
Then calmly tells me
"Have a strong will"
I go to visit her
Almost every day
And she always has something
Sad to say

"I have a bump on my right side
Another on my left
One under my breast
And yet two on my back
Still two on my head
And with them there
I'll soon be dead
Be strong, David"
She tells me this...
"Try and hold tight
For while the others ran
You stood to fight"
These words I hear
Over in my brain
Sometimes I think
"I'm going insane!"
Her pain hits me deep
Deep in my heart
For I know that too soon
We'll be apart
As the others try
To outrun the night
Here I stand alone
One single light

"Special Time"

If I could stop
Her pain
I would.
If I could change
Places with her
I would.
If she would only smile
It would be easier on me
But I know how it will be.
I try to enjoy her
While I can
But it hurts.
It hurts me
To see her hurt
It makes me cry
To see her cry.
When I want to
Tell the truth
I tell a lie.

I try to protect her
From the pain
Although my tears
Flow in vain.
Now all can do
Is stay with her
And try to understand her.
Now time has passed
And all that there is left
For me to do is...

...Remember her the way
She wanted me to
Instead of the pain
She went through.

"You and I"

Time and time again
And yet another day
I say this to you
With no further delay
"If you'll be my guiding light
Through that darkening door
And onward through life
Forever more
I'll be whomever and whatever
You want me to be
From now
Unto eternity
We've gone through Hell
On this earth together
And we'll do so
For ever and thereafter
We've made it this far
Though times have changed
Like the Heavenly stars above
Turned into hellish
Red balls of flames
As they did
When Satan came
Like the angel you are
On this Christmas holiday
You've brightened my life
In a very special way

"Your Day"

On this Sunday
This twelfth of May
You're to be honored
For the things you've done
For everyone
You're the Mom
Whom we do love
And we'll do so
For all the days to come

HAPPY MOTHER'S DAY

Father's Eyes
(Prayer time)

"A Friend In Need"

While walking near
The cool river shore
The Lord came to me.

We walked a while
Then came to rest
Under the shade
Of an oak tree.

There my heart
Was set soarin'
My prayers were blessed

He asked what
I had to say
I said, "I have a friend,
Who seems shut away."
He said, "I've come to you,
So we could pray.
So that your friend,
Will search for me.
To find the way."

"Dear Lord,"
I continued to say,
"I don't know what's wrong,
He will not say,
Or let me help him along."

There we sat,
The Lord and me.
He asked, "Has your friend come to thee?"

I replied,
"I've prayed and prayed,
For him to do so.
But day by day,
Further apart we go.
Please Lord,
I say this to You.
Please let him know,
That things will get better,
Once he's found you."

"Angel From Heaven"

Today I saw...

A lonely man walking aimlessly down a meadow path,
The man's head hung low upon his shoulders. He thought the
path lead to nowhere, but this one guided him somewhere.
From the Heavens and through the tree tops a ray of sun fell to
the ground.
The man's head moved upward as his knee bent. He prayed.
Moments after, a young lady stood where the light touched the
earth. Tears fell from his eyes.

"Who are you?" He asked.

"I am Mary. Do you not believe in the Lord Jesus?"

"Well, I have not thought of believing in Him. Why are
you here?" He asked, still on one knee.

"I, my son, have come to deliver you from the depths of
hell and Satan's hold. Stand and walk. As you walk, pray.
Continue to pray and at the end of the path you will feel that
your depression has lifted."

"How do you know this?" he wondered.

"Ye of little faith. I promise, it is true."

The lonely man closed his eyes, thinking, and when he opened
them she was gone. He walked on as he had been told.
Finding what she said to be true. His depression was gone.
He turned and a dove was where he was on bended knee.
When the dove rose, so did the night's shadows.
He raised his eyes to heaven, saying to himself, *How did this
Mary know I was low in Spirit?*
He was no longer the lonely man. That was the day Jesus
sent an angel into his sight.

"Angels Unaware"

An arm grabs hold
A fist cocked
The blade went in
I should have dropped

Arm held up
In a blood soaked coat
Skin turned gray
I started to float

Pain wasn't felt
The cut not seen
Anger flowing
Questions going

Someone's eyes
Burned into my head
If it wasn't for them
I would be dead

Satan Lost

Thank God
For unexpected friends

"Before I Go"

Turn around
Don't shut Him out forever
If there's a chance
The slightest chance
Never say never

You know it's out of your hands
'Cause you're in way over your head
Blink
And He'll be there
In your dark oversight

There must be a last breath
Of a relationship
If there's something I can say
To make you see His way
Just tell me
Before I go

There's an angel inside
Could you please release him

Is it a crime
To surrender to His love?
Maybe I've tried too hard
To help you see the way

It won't take long
If there's something I can say
To make you see His way
Just tell me
Before I go

I don't know where
Your road will end
Nor the die hard resistance

I'll wait
He's waiting
Someday you'll see the Son

"Christ, I Know"

From time to time
I've called for Him
I never thought He heard
But now I know
He'll always hear
I've asked Him into my heart
With Him near and so close to me
I know I've found happiness
With Him there

Christ, My Savior
I have found a home
This home will never fill with sadness

I shall never feel the shadows of night
Coming to crowd my day
I will always feel the glory of His might
Guiding me the right way

If ever I shed a tear in sadness
I know He'll lift me out of the fear
And take me to where I'll see the way clear

"Dear Lord, Thank You"

Dear Lord,

I know You're listening,
To what I have,
To say.
Thank You, Lord,
For guiding me,
This way.
I knew that You,
Were calling me.
Though I thought it,
Not to be true.
I have learned,
Through the help,
Of my loved ones.
To hold my trust,
In You.

For without Your love,
To guide me.
I would not have,
Found the way.
And also at this time,
This very night.
I've taken the time,
To say,
Thank You, Lord,
For finding my brother's wife,
And he.
For they are the loved ones,
That have brought You closer to me.

"Facing Up"

A voice
I heard
"My son,
I would not ask you to do this.
Why?"

******

A silent prayer I cried
"Dear God,
I don't want to die."
Cut cleaned
Sewn and covered
The anger's gone
But for how long?

******

I saw tears in your eyes
When all was done
You saw anger in mine
When this first began

You were going to hit me
That I was told
I wish you had
Knocked me out cold

******

We talked of differences
Between religion
And Relations
One thing we believe is
Satan is the enemy
Keep smilin'

******

You wanted to move
I wouldn't blame you if you did
We spoke of this issue
Death before 26

******

Anyone have a blade?
(Joke)

"Flying Alone"

I saw him walking swiftly in front of me. He was like a bird
flying to get away from a bird catcher.
I walked a few feet behind. We were headed for the lunch
room. The aroma of French Fries filled my nose, making me
want to taste them, even though I didn't want them.
I heard him say to someone behind him, words that could have
been meant for me. My ears seemed to reach out and grab
those words. I could hear and feel what he said more clearly.
I was a bird-watcher watching a bird as he flew back outside. I
followed, with hopes that I might catch him long enough to say
"hi", but I stopped solid in my tracks.
I watched as his pace quickened and he flew towards the
gathering of trees in the distance. I wondered if he'd ever
understand the differences Christ has made in my life. Would
I ever see him again?

"Friends Rust"

Here I am
Lost in all confusion
Now I don't know what to do
Here I am
Standing in the rain
Friends rust
When it rains on friendships
Thunder rolls in on our
Clear blue days
Our friendship use to shine
Like the sun in the sky
Something happened
The weather changed
I should have known better
We were too close
We had something
We weren't able to hold on to
Friends rust

When it rains on friendships
Hailstones fall heavy
On the memory of our start
They cloud the window
Where we use to be friends
That goes to show
Some friendships do end
Friends rust
When it rains on friendships
Thunder rolls in on our
Clear blue days
Our friendship use to shine
Like the sun in the sky
Something happened
The weather changed

When the storm's over
Will our friendship shine?

"Give Me The Strength"

My friend in need still worries me so
I thought it would be okay
When the semester ended
I knew I wouldn't see him every day

Having it this way
Was fine with me
While I was at home
His pain no longer hurt me
At this time my worries were at ease

Then one day while walking near the wash
Where the water ran smoothly
I thought of the new semester
And if we should meet

The semester began and he was back
The worries arrived like a heart attack
He's hurting inside
This I can see
Would he confide in me?

Please give me the strength
To ask what is wrong
He has not a glance to be given
Or a word to be said

He's given me the feeling
That he's dead
I realize he's not
He walks around campus alive and okay
Except when he walks my way

Please give me the strength to make the Word known
Or give the me the strength to let it go

"God's Child"

His voice:

I'll lend you for a little time
A child of mine," He said
"For you to love, the while he lives
And mourn for when he's dead."

"He may be two or seven
Or twenty-two or three
But, will you, till I call him back
Take care of him for me?"

"He'll bring his charms to gladden you
And should his day be brief
You'll have his lonely memories
As solace for your grief."

"I can't promise he will stay
Since all on earth return
But there are lessons taught on earth
I want this child to learn."

I've looked this wide world over
In search of teachers true
And from the throngs that crowd life's love
I have selected you."

"Now will you give him all your love
Nor think the labor vain?
Nor hate me when I come to call
To take him back again?"

I fancied that I heard them say:

Parents reply:
"Dear Lord, Thy will be done."

"For all the joy thy child shall bring
The risk of grief we'll run
We'll shelter him with tenderness
We'll love him while we may
And for the happiness we've known
Forever grateful stay."

"But should the angels call for him
Much sooner than we've planned
We'll brave the bitter grief that comes
We'll try to understand."

"I Walk 'Alone'"

Many people who walk on the beach,
Walk hand in hand.

I always walk,
(From what they see),
Alone.

People think they see,
A person staring aimlessly,
Out towards the sea.
I'm not alone,
Not me.

If those people knew that person who's alone,
They'd know that he is never alone.
The Lord walks beside him.

The Lord talks with him of things,
No one else will hear.
He understands.

When I sit 'alone' at the edge,
Where the water meets the sand,

I think:

People may have the love of another,
To keep them warm.

They may not have what I have.
I may not have an earthly person to lean on,
But the Lord Jesus, from above;
Will keep me warm and give me inner strength,
While we sit together.
My hand in His hand.

"Jesus"

Jesus is the man
Everyone
Seeks
Under the
Sun

"Jesus' Light A-Rose"

Yesterday, Today and Forever

There are two ways in which Jesus and a rose are the same:

Hold Jesus' light and a rose up
And they both look beautiful.
Feed Jesus with praise
And the rose with water
They shall both stand for you

There are two ways in which they differ:

Through time, when you look up at the rose
In Jesus' light, to help you when you're low
In spirit, it will be faded and gone.
But, look beyond the wilting flower
To Jesus' light, to help you when you're low
in spirit, and you'll feel Him
Never faded-Never gone
For He's as strong as when you first held Him up

The rose is here today, gone tomorrow
Jesus is here Yesterday, Today and Forever!

"Light and Dark"

The sun
Shines for
All those who live
In the love
That the Lord
Has to give

Those around
Care for you
But there's nothing
We can do
It's your life
It's up to you

We also get high
But not like you
Instead of drugs
We get high on life
And the love
From Jesus above

"Lord, Come to Me"

In my time of need,
Lord, come to me.
I need you now,
I need to see
Why do I wander,
Away from Your word?
I do know,
You need to be heard.
Lord, come to me.
Lead my back,
It is You,
Who keeps me on track.

"Lord, Thy Father, In the Sky"

I have to say these words on paper
For I'm not too good at saying them in prayer
Though I don't know why I do it this way
I see You every day

You're in the clear blue waters
That sounds of maidens crying
You're in the soft wind's blow
You're in the hearts of babies
And with them as they grow

I'm sorry that You were to die
To give us eternal life

I'm sorry for my sins

The Word I want
To share

Thank You Lord, for showing us the Light

"Lord's Heaven"

Leader
Of
Righteous
Deliverance
Safely to

Happiness that's
Everyone's
After saying
Victorious prayers
Everlasting in His
Name

(Without Christ you could be...)
"Lost In A Crowd"

Isn't it weird how you can meet a person
get to know him so good that you become close?
So close it's sometimes scary. Or so it seems.
But when one leaves to have time alone,
he comes back to find things have changed.

I've experienced a time such as this.
It's peculiar. When I returned from having time
alone, I found that my friend had changed.
We both changed. I didn't really know him
and he didn't want to know me.

For this I am sorry.

The friend I once knew, was special.
Now he's just another face...

Lost in a crowd.

"Meet Me Half Way"

Lord,

Meet me half way.
Across the sky.
My world belongs,
To You now.

Meet me half way,
And help me to try.
It's with You
I want to fly.

Meet me half way,
As time goes by.
Give me the strength,
So I will never lie.

Meet me half way,
Across the land.
When we meet,
Please take my hand.

Meet me half way,
Across the sea.
You are the one,
Who has set me free.

"My Room"

A place a majesty
A prison
A place free of confusion and insanity
Yet the walls crawl inward toward me
Space I can call my own
When everyone else's space is blown
Privacy never to be disturbed
Yet if I don't get out
I'll be corrupted
A place where I'm condemned
Without a doubt
Time spent here
Is time to think
Soaking up the wall's
Knowledge and stories
Help, I need to be freed
My room seems humble
When I'm away
But I know
When I'm behind the door
I'm there for a never-ending stay

"Oh God, You Devil"

You woke one day   Thinking that there's
Dirty deeds to be done   But now there's only
One way
This is the day   You signed
Your life away
Here comes Satan   Knocking at your door
You were once nice   Since you've met him
You've been rotten to the core
Play the game
Because the devil
Deals the cards
Sleep late   Forget your responsibilities
You've got a date   A date with death
Midnight sharp
You'll sniff, drink   And pop till you drop
By Grace you awaken
To find a surprise   The Lord God
Stands in your room   Trying to stop you
From doing your doom
Jesus met with Satan   In the casino place
He talked of saving   The human race
He dealt the cards   This one last time
To keep Satan   From committing a crime
If our Lord wins
Satan loses the play   He'll turn and flee
And you'll be free   To live another day

"One Empty Room"

One night, one empty room.
One Man's got His mind on you.

I made a wish.
It didn't come true.

You never answered.,
When He called your name.

It's hard to admit,
But the truth remains:
Our friendship's over.

I'm holding on,
Not letting go.
Please,
What's wrong,
Let me know.

Sometimes I see myself as you.
I know I'm wasting my time.
No one can take your place.
I close my eyes,
And see your face.
Open them,
And you're gone.

All this time I've been drowning,
In the hopeless illusion,
That one day you'll walk,
Out of the shadows...
Into the Light.

"Privacy of Your Room"

Look at what you've done to me,
Even though you're not around.
God will give you promises.
He'll hold you up,
When you are down.
If you're willing to learn,
Then take a tip from me.
Don't turn your back,
On His word.
He promises to help you,
During the times when things go wrong.
In the privacy of your room,
If you talk to Him,
He'll answer you.
He's knocking at your heart.
Listen... hear...
And open the door.
You'll be lonely never more.
He promises to be with you,
As you face the trials of life.
Don't lean on your own understanding,
But trust in Him--the Light.
In the privacy of your room,
If you ask Him to,
He'll lift you from the night.

"Special Relationship"

Your relationship is special to me
It gets the anger and sadness
I hold, free
I pray our relationship
Never ends
I want it to last
Until for me
Your Father sends
With our relationship
I'll cover the past
But not all the way
In hopes that the future
Comes in clearer
I sometimes feel
The end is here
But with you
I'll end my fear
You are the light
To this relationship
And the Light is the life
To which I'll hold on
May it grow
Forever strong

"Take Them Away"

Take them away;
To Your home above
Where the clouds are white
With trims of love

Take the away;
Where spirits run free
Like Angels galore
They want to live there
Forever more

Take them away;
Where Your glory always shines
Where time never stops
And there are no tick-tocks

Take them away;
Where Your music is heard
An no one speaks an unkind word

Take them away;
In the darkness of night
Or in the brightness of day
Come for them soon
So they may be found

Take them away;
Those lost souls
Down here who walk the ground

Take them away;
So they may live in Your love
And no longer in pain

"We Are As Children In The Dark"

WE ARE AS CHILDREN IN THE DARK
Trying not to be afraid
Together we'll grow strong
And accept what is wrong

Although it's okay
To cry
Try and hold your head high

And when the shadows subside
You'll no longer have to hide
Your sadness deep inside

WE ARE AS CHILDREN IN THE DARK
Trying no to be afraid
Together we'll grow strong
And accept what is wrong.

"You Are"

You are the sun,
the moon.
You are the mountains,
the seas.
You are the universe,
the earth.
You are the human heart,
Which beats with life.
You are the glory,
Seen after death.
You are the stars,
Which grace the skies.
You are my strength,
During hard times and struggling tries.

"You Try To Hide"

You want to run,
You want to hide.
You think the truth will go away,
So you won't have to decide.
He wants you here,
He wants you to know.
Just search, and you'll find the way.
He'll say what He will.
You're living in a dream.
Please do what He wants.
You keep turning away,
So you won't hear,
What He'll say.
'Cause you're not sure,
What you should do.
You make me look at you,
The way you used to be.
But I know your heart,
Will someday see.
You will never be blinded.
Just let go,
Of the feeling that pulls at your heart.
Talk to Him,
And if you have to go,
He'll go with you.

"You Were There"

All along
I knew that
You were there
When times got rough
I got tough
When my friends were weak
I was strong
There's lots
To thank You for
I don't know
Where to start
When my days were darkened
You helped me see the light
The only words to say
That will make it seem
All right
Thank You, Lord
For showing me the light

"Your Decision"

You've already made up your mind.
You know who you're not looking for,
And what kind of life you'll find.

I'm trying to live in reality,
Since you've shut Him out,
You're living in a fantasy.

I won't ruin your plans,
But, please find His hand.
Tomorrow doesn't matter today,
Unless you let yourself go,
And search out His way.

I really hate to see you confused.
Give Him a try,
You've got nothing to lose.
Give your life to Him,
You'll see it's right.
Then I won't have to hold on,
To your memory so tight.

Satan's Chamber
(Don't go there)

"Nuclear War"

I'm the Global Nuclear War.
In just minutes,
Over the earth,
My killer gasses will soar.
I'm the most powerful one,
Of them all.
With a smile I'll watch,
All your bodies fall.

The only way,
To survive my wrath,
Is to have a place under ground,
And stay there for a year.
Waiting for my raging gasses to clear.
If you don't do,
What I've suggested above,
Say good-bye
To those you love.

When I've come,
Covering the sky.
All you'll hear,
Is their one last cry.
All those,
Who walk on this earth,
Will die.

I'll be happy,
For all I've done.
For there's no survivors.
Not even one.

Ha!   Ha!   I have won.
For it's my grip,
Even your souls,
Can't out run.

"Satan Won"

I knew the war
Was going to come
So there was no need to run
I got a knife
Sharpened the blade
Went to my room
Pulled down the shade
Through my shirt
Man does it hurt
The blade is in deep
I start to weep
I fell to the floor
With a loud bang
Out of my mouth
Came words of slang
My eyes closed
As blood flowed
My soul then stood
Next to my body
And from the windows
Of my soul
I saw my body
Lying there
This was my end
I may have won the battles
But Satan won this war

"When I'm Gone"

I've lived a life
Of sixteen years
Some of happiness
Some of tears
Though my death
May come slow or fast
I've lived a memorable past
I've hurt my family
And my friends
So I shall
Bring their pain
To an end
With my passing away
They will live
Painless days
When I'm gone
Life will go on
Chad watches from above
In God's house of love
I will be below
Dancing with fire
On white hot coals
Sorry God
To Satan I gave in

Friendships Forever
(Run with the memories)

"A Good Friend"

Good friends are rare.
When you find one,
He's always there.
He'll keep you out of trouble,
With the law.
And away from drugs,
And alcohol.
He's there when you need him.
And even when you think you don't.
He'll share your joy,
Your sorrows, too.
He cares for you ,
And you care for him too.
He'll watch out for you.
Like a guardian angel,
Wherever you look,
He's there.

Although you may drive him insane,
He remembers the good times,
And sometimes laughs at the pain.
He's someone with whom,
You get along.
He'll straighten you out,
When things go wrong.
He'll listen,
Not saying a word.
Give you advice,
When it's his turn.

Remember...

He may not be God, but he's a true friend.

"A Walk On The Beach"

As the waves roll
Upon the sand
I wish you would
Try to understand
The love for you
Rolls in my heart
I know that your habit
Will tear us apart
All I can do
Is hold on tight
For what you're doing
Is an awful sight
As we walk hand-in-hand
Fingers intertwined
I try and see
What's going through your mind
As the sun sets low
On the sea's horizon
I know you hurt
But I'll keep trying
For if your life ends
Because of your "flying"
I will go on
But only to keep crying

"Double Image"

You live a double life
You may not see it
But those around you can

We tried to make you understand

Think of your children
They're reason enough
To stop taking
That stuff

Without your high
Kind of friends
Life never ends

Someone special
Loves you a lot
But you've got him
On the spot

You care for drugs
And the boy next door
Better than the one
Who loves you more

Give your children
The life you never had
You said you could
Raise them without
A dad

Enter slowly
This world He lives on
But make sure
The drugs are gone

He loves you
For who you are
And when you're
On drugs
He loves you
From afar

Live for your kids
If not for me

Live for them
If not for Him

Give your life to Jesus
Before it is too late

"Hendrix"

I've known you since
Eighty-two
Since then
You've been true
Like a brother
I care for you
You were there
When I needed someone to talk to
Growing up wasn't easy
We fought for a friendship
That wasn't supposed to be
But I never gave up on you
You never gave up on me
From Buckner's Ranch
To Marble Falls
I received letters
But no phone calls

I enjoyed them then
Where are they now?

"Maverick"

I left home
In eighty-six
Never looking back
Never saying good-bye
Now, eight years later
I'm wondering why
Miles have increased
The distance between us is vast
But memories keep us
Connected to the past
You grew up fast
You never got mean
Oh, and a daddy, too
I thought I'd never live
To see it happen to you
I promised to return
To keep it
I still yearn
One day we'll meet again
Though apart we have grown
Brothers we'll remain

"Mechelle"

You're the friend
On whom I once
Had a crush
But it soon
Turned to lust
When you told me
You wanted to be free
It was then
I did see
That the love
You held for me
Was only brotherly
As a sister now
I'll think of you
As for the love
That's more than family
It should go gradually

"September 1986"

In September * I met a beautiful older woman
She held her youth well * At first I thought it wasn't true
All my adventures * Would involve her
A day came to pass * When we met face to face
Something clicked * Was there something there?
At least in my wildest dreams * As time passed
We grew to know each other * We laughed, cried
Plastered on rum balls during lunch
We cheated on tests * We laughed even more
It was great * The relationship took off
We became close * She saw me
As a son * We became closer still
Like twins we began to feel
She felt my pain and laughter * As I felt hers
We leaned on one another * More than once
We thought for each other * Finishing sentences
"When we bad..." "...We good."
I look back now * And see the beautiful person
I grew to love * We may not have a lover's relationship
It's better * Trust, Respect and honesty between friends
No matter how far we are * Or large the states are
that separate us * I will always be thankful to God
For that day in September 1986

Mystical Creations
(Daydream if you wish)

"A Unicorn's Flight Within A Dream"

There once was a unicorn,
Named Thunder.
He was the brightest white,
All under.
He lived in the forest,
Where he thought was the most boring.
It wasn't where he wanted to be,
But he had nowhere else to go.
While he walked in the sun-lit snow,
He said to himself, "Oh, how I wish I could fly into
the light blue sky."

In the forest,
Where he lay,
He looked up at the moon while it glistened upon
the snow.
As he lay the next night,
He found he'd give anything to fly off on a night flight.

In his dreams,
In spite of everything,
He grew wings,
And then he flew into the moon-lit silvery night.

"Medusa"

I seen my body,
Turn to stone.
When Medusa's face.
Had been shown.
Her hair was changed,
To real large snakes.
One look at her,
And my life,
She did take.
But my soul is set free,
For out of my body,
It did come.
During the few seconds,
Of breath I had in me,
Through the windows,
Of my soul,
I could see.
What was happening to me?
There my body stood.
In the last position,
It took.
Though my body is now dead,
My soul does live.
It remembers,
What my eyes were fed.

"The Night I Met A Unicorn"

It was the night before summer,
Oh, a peaceful night.
When out of the star-lit sky,
Came a unicorn in flight.
He landed on earth,
Saying to himself, "Good, I was the first to arrive."
He walked a little to his right,
Then he came toward me,
In the middle of the night.
He asked, "Is this the planet where animals like me,
Can come to be free?"
I answered, "Yes, here you can be as free as you can
possibly be."
We became friends after a while.
One day we took a walk to the Nile.
I looked into his eyes and found,
They were a bright shade of blue.
That night was so clear,
Although we knew the time was too near.
The night soon came,
When the unicorn flew off on a beautiful flight,
Into the moon-lit silvery night

"What is a Unicorn?"

What is a unicorn?
Is she loving, sweet and beautiful,
Or is she a savage ugly beast?
But, when you see her,
She seems to sweep you off your feet.
To me, I think unicorns are really,
Really neat.
They are symbols of love,
Are they not?
They have fought for their lives,
And freedom,
Just as we have fought.
Are they a myth,
Or are they real?
Anyway, that is how I feel.

His Gifts
(I love you, boys)

(Joshua)
"I'll Never Forget the Joy You Bring"

Sunrise by day
Each night I pray
I hear your laughter
I see your face
Your zest for life
Is my heart's embrace
In my heart
You're love
I'll hold
God's gift of you
Is priceless
I know

I love you, son

William
"Mirror Image"

When this child is born
I will make you feel
Love in troubled times
Laughter instead of pain
In his eyes you'll see
A likeness to you
May he bring you closer to she

(I held you in my arms, I prayed these words.)

"Unborn"

This unborn
Is now a life form
Which is a very special
Part of you
This baby is someone you'll
Love and care for
From the time of conception
Until time is no more
Within you a child grows
A girl
A boy
Only God knows
Take care of this gift
Cherish the laughter
Bare the tears
Give thanks to God
Enjoy the years

"Why is it always darkest before the dawn?"

Before the sun set
And dark shadows appear
His heart cried out
For his child to hear
The demons arrived
Blackness fell hard
Away went his child
With his child went his heart
In the distance
The hours past
Tear drops fell
In a painful
Bloody crash
Years go as the day breaks
Evil murkiness stays
He smiles with laughter
His heart aches
No child to raise
No "Daddy" phrase
No first step taken
No first word spoken
Just a clip-on tie
As a small token

Will the dawn ever come?

Knots in this Family
(Members only)

"A Phone Call"

Last night I received a call from my sister in Minnesota. She was so excited that I was coming to live in a state, that when the temperature reaches fifty degrees above zero, it's hot.

The snow is gone and life has gone on since I left. I too am excited about going, but not as excited as she. She doesn't know what I'm giving up to go.

A family with many problems that have yet to be resolved. A family that has love too make up with and cover the scars of their fights.

The warm state of California: it's sandy white beaches, green-blue oceans, the cry of sea gulls in the air and the cries of the baby that has brought this family together.

My school, where I have been given the chance to open the door to my goal as a writer and friends that were there when she wasn't.

She only sees what I can only think of:

Time well spent with the other part of my large family. The new friends I will make and those who await my return. The chance to further my education. Most of all, she sees that I am very close too achieving my dream as a writer. She knows that I will be happy there, as I am here.

She doesn't know however...

Just how much I will miss the state I once wanted never to return to.

As we went to hang up, she said, "See ya in a few weeks."

All I said was, ""Bye."

"A Year In October"

In October,
It will be a year.
Since you've gone,
We've shed tears.
Not of happiness,
But of pain.
For you've gone,
To the Lord's house,
Of no vain.
Though your time came,
On one October night.
You have no need,
To show your hidden fright.
For now you watch over us,
With your light so bright.
Don't show sadness or fear,
For you're in the hands,
Of the Man,
So dear.

You brought this family,
Happiness and joy,
For you are a lovely little boy.
For three months and six days,
You lived on this earth,
Not yet covered with snow.
But now onward,
Our lives must go.
Along with us,
Your memory goes, too.
So remember this,
For this I may say:
We'll always love you!
For ever and a day!

"Cabin"

The cabin,
During those summer months,
Four years ago...

The ground was covered in white fluffy snow.
The purity vanished,
Replaced by mud puddles and sludge.
The leaves were seen,
In a flash on a movie screen.
Down the trees came,
And a home was to be.
Though it was dark at night,
With no bright lights.
The peacefulness boomed,
With no television or ringing phone,
To break the deafening silence.
Making the best,
Of what we had.
Was a lesson taught to a child,
From his Dad.
I'll remember this small log place.
It was a great place to learn,
And a great place to play.

"Chad"

The grass is green.
The roads are worn.
It's over you I still mourn.
The sun may shine bright,
Over this land.
It is God
Who has you in His hand.
In the month of July,
You got a sister.
She looks like you,
Or so I've heard.
But I wouldn't know,
My memory of you,
Is kind of blurred.
It's hard to believe,
That it's been a year.
Every now and again,
I shed a tear.
Especially when I think,
Of back then.
Once in a while,
When I see your sister,
I call her Chad.
Although that's not her name,
It can't be that bad.
It just shows,
I'm thinking of you.

"Just Me"

On my own
I've realized
That I have grown
Though what I do
May be wrong
It will be the mistake
I've learned not to make
All I ask of you
Is to understand
And listen with a prayer at hand
If I could reach
As high and as far
As the Northern Star
Then maybe I'd find myself
In a clearer state of mind
No more confusion
Or Satan's temptation
And expose myself
To what lay ahead
And be free
With Jesus guiding me

"Pictures"

Memories are pictures,
Jumbled in your head.

Pictures of happiness, sadness,
Or of a father you wish was dead.
Places, things and friends to the end.
Triumphs cut short,
Succeeding at last.

Pictures of Chad;
The dimples filled with laughter.
A life stopped suddenly,
No happily ever after.

Pictures of times when differences weren't seen
And friends were abundant and close.
Life was slow, for the future was ours to dream.

Pictures of walks in the park,
Swimming after dark.
First kisses,
Blackouts with swinging fists.
Busted windows and dented walls,
From a body who should have seen.
What he saw.

To heck with the pictures,
Jumbled in my head.
I am now a father,
I sometimes wish I was dead.

"The Unwanted"

Living alone
I wish I could be
Instead of behind
These bars
Of captivity

I am a burden
To everyone
That I wish
Not to be

My step-dad says
That I am to blame
For all their pain

I wish to go
So far away
So that he
Won't have anything
To say

"Through the Years"

He stayed by,
To watch me grow up.
Even when we were apart,
He was always in my heart.
When I was in another state,
He wrote to me,
Without a sign of hate.
He took care of me,
In times of trouble.
He stood by to catch me,
When I started to stumble.
When things went wrong,
He helped me along.

"What Is A Childhood?"

A LIFETIME that once was lived
But will never be lived again
A LIFETIME filled with hopes for the future
Yet full of memories to forget
A LIFETIME in the past
That went too fast at times;
Too slow at others
A LIFETIME filled with sunshine for some
And darkness for others
A LIFETIME to be stuffed in a file cabinet
And never pulled out
A LIFETIME that is lived
By those who abuse, hate, love and care

MISCELANEOUS
(Where do we fit in?)

"Covering Up Fear"

Rainy days are like blankets,
That hide the tears,
That are shed in fear.

Blankets cover you,
To hide those creatures,
In the night,
That bring out,
Your hidden fright.

The gray clouds,
That cover the skies,
Are like the eyelids,
That cover your eyes.

There's a rainbow in the rain.
Like the laughter,
Blocking out the pain.

"Don't Drink and Drive"

Don't drink,
And Drive,
If you want to stay alive.
Drink to your taste,
But don't let life,
Go to waste.
If you do drink,
More than you think,
Call someone you know,
To drive you home.
Just call on us,
Because we care.
We'll be there.

"Minnesota Is Like A Prison, Texas Is The Key"

Minnesota is like a prison cell.
With the breath-taking beautiful snow,
And the freezing cold,
Acting as a mysterious spell.

Texas is the key,
That will open the bars,
Of these cold open arms.

Give me a week,
Or two,
Maybe even three,
And the sight of Texas will set me free.

"(My Son) Life Will Go On"

You're the child,
My girlfriend had.
She is your mother,
And I am your dad.

Your mother is gone,
But you're the one,
She loved so.
Onward your life,
Must go.

I have my memories,
Of a love,
She and I shared.
And you were conceived,
Because we cared.

I cried so hard.
It was sad.
I only wish,
She could have held,
The boy she had.

You came early,
Into this world.
Now around my finger,
Your fingers do curl.

I'll love you forever,
Which is longer than I can show or say.
It is with me,
You will stay.

You bring sunshine,
Over the tears.
Son, Daddy will always care.
I will always be there

"Rain"

Rain drops,
Are tears,
From Heaven.

Like those,
From your eyes.

Only these come
From the skies.

Your tears,
Are as those,
From heaven.

Which are of truth,
And not of lies.

"So Long Minnesota"

Moving day is here,
Flying in a plane,
Opens my fears.
We have people to see,
Things to do,
And places to be.
We're going to Texas,
My home state.
I can't wait!
Away from this freezing cold,
I am not.
But give me three and a half hours,
Then the Texan heat,
I'll hold.